Magnificent Messina
A Kid's Guide To Messina, Sicily, Italy

Photography by John D. Weigand
Poetry by Penelope Dyan

Bellissima Publishing, LLC
Jamul, California
www.bellissimapublishing.com

Copyright © 2016 by Penny D. Weigand and John D. Weigand

All rights reserved. No part of this book may be reproduced or transmitted in any form or by any means, electronic or mechanical, including photocopying, recording, or by any other means, or by any information or storage retrieval system, without permission from the publisher.

ISBN 978-1-61477-260-6
First Edition

"It is not in the stars to hold our destiny but in ourselves."

WILLIAM SHAKESPEARE

Introduction

Messina, is the capital of Sicily. Founded by the Greeks, it has a long history of having to rebuild itself, giving a strength to its inhabitants, who do not readily give in to any adversity as a people. In 1783, an earthquake destroyed much of the city. It took decades to rebuild. Another earthquake damaged the city on November 16, 1894, and Messina was almost entirely destroyed by an earthquake and tsunami. December 28, 1908, that killed approximately 60,000 people and destroyed most of its ancient architecture. The city was rebuilt in the following year. Then there was further damage from massive Allied air bombardments in 1943, during World War II.

But this book is not about that, this book is about how all these things impacted and shaped the minds and souls of the people of Messina, Sicily; and this is the real story behind the story.

Practice reading skills through word recognition, and through word repetition and rhyme, and think about Messina's people. Try to imagine the place of antiquity founded by the Greeks and then see more of this place as you watch the free music video that goes with this book, posted on the Bellissimavideo YouTube channel.

Magnificent Messina
Bellissima Publishing, LLC

Magnificent Messina
A Kid's Guide To Messina, Sicily, Italy

Photography by John D. Weigand
Poetry by Penelope Dyan

In Messina, Sicily,
the earthquakes came;
and as the ground began to rumble,
the buildings there
began to crumble.

In came a tsunami,
dashing against the shore.
The people of Messina,
rebuilt their grand city once more.
Together they faced destruction
and strife.
Working together
they rebuilt their lives.

This church,
Annunziata del Catalani,
stands as a symbol to the people,
on its original ground,
while the buildings around it crumbled,
in a great, thunderous sound.

There is a museum in Messina,*
and outside (in the yard) sit five bells
and some other things.

* Museo Regionale Interdisciplinare di Messina

Silent the bells sit.
Not one of them rings.

Inside is a crucifix, Jesus Christ hanging on the cross. Christians stop and stare, contemplating life and loss.

And there is a painting of
the Christ child and his mother,*
that you decide is like no other.
Can it be you have seen this face,
full of love and full of grace?

*Girolamo Alibrandi, Circoncisione

Next to the Cathedral Basilica
there stands a tower,
and on this clock you check
the time and the hour.
This is the Orologio Astronomico,
the largest astronomical clock
in the world!
So you look up, and you wait,
for the countdown to be unfurled.

Inside the Cathedral Basilica,
stained glass, chandeliers and candles
light the way;
and many worshipers stop
to kneel and to pray.

There's a museum and a bookshop here
that you can stop and see.
How much more interesting and fun
could anyplace possibly be?

You contemplate a painting.
You study a Roman Soldier's face.
His eyes want to tell you a story,
all about this place.
And you know VERY well,
that if pictures could talk,
a long story he'd tell

Outside once again, a fountain is seen.*
Behind it tree leaves form a backdrop,
a dark blanket of green.

* Fontana di Orione

Then as from magnificent Messina,
you walk sadly away,
you think about the lessons
you have learned this day,
about perseverance, about rebuilding,
about faith and about trust. .
about how overcoming life's obstacles,
is an absolute must.
And you realize there's only one thing
that you really need,
and that's faith
the size of a mustard seed!

"And Jesus said unto them, 'Because of your unbelief: for verily I say unto you, If ye have faith as a grain of mustard seed, ye shall say unto this mountain, Remove hence to yonder place; and it shall remove; and nothing shall be impossible unto you.'"

Matthew 17:20
King James Version
Holy Bible

www.ingramcontent.com/pod-product-compliance
Ingram Content Group UK Ltd.
Pitfield, Milton Keynes, MK11 3LW, UK
UKHW060136240426

12048UKWH00002B/60